SALES, INVENTORY AND SUCCESS

A Merchant's Guide to Financial Clarity and Growth

CA Sukanya Dilip Halyal

notionpress.com

INDIA • SINGAPORE • MALAYSIA

ISBN
Paperback 979-8-90584-416-4
Hardcase 979-8-90584-417-1

Contents

Acknowledgements

This book represents a significant milestone in my eight years of practice as a Chartered Accountant, and it would not have been possible without the unwavering support of many individuals.

First and foremost, I offer my deepest gratitude to my **late father, Dilip Halyal**. Though he is no longer with us, his presence is felt in every chapter of my life. His values of integrity, discipline and hard work are the very foundation upon which my career is built. I know his blessings continue to guide me, and I hope this work serves as a tribute to the legacy he left behind.

To my **mother, Megha Halyal**, thank you for your unwavering strength, immense patience and for being my constant support while I balanced my practice and my writing.

A special note of gratitude to my **family and friends**, who have always stood by me with encouragement and warmth.

To **my Business Mentor, Mr. Gaurav Arora**, thank you for being the one who saw the "Author" in me before I did. Your belief that I could write this book was the catalyst I needed to begin.

Finally, to my **Clients,** the wholesalers, distributors and retailers. Thank you for trusting me with your business "Data" and your growth over the last eight years. This book is for you.

Foreword

Through our business journey, I have had the opportunity to interact with several traders, distributors, retailers, and business owners across India. While every business is different, one challenge appears again and again—businesses focus heavily on increasing sales but often do not have the systems or financial visibility needed to convert those sales into sustainable profits.

In a family business, we have always believed that growth must be supported by discipline, systems, and a clear understanding of numbers. Sustainable success is built not only on strong sales but also on efficient operations, prudent financial management, and the ability to make informed decisions at the right time.

Many entrepreneurs work extremely hard. Their sales are growing, their customer base is expanding, and yet they frequently find themselves struggling with cash flow, excess inventory, delayed collections, or uncertainty about the actual profitability of their business. In my experience, these issues arise not because of a lack of effort, but because critical business decisions are often taken without adequate financial information.

This is where ***Sales, Inventory and Success*** make a meaningful contribution.

CA Sukanya Dilip Halyal brings together her years of professional experience working closely with small and medium-sized businesses and presents it in a practical and easy-to-understand manner. Rather than discussing finance in complex technical terms, she explains how business owners can use their own numbers to make better decisions, improve inventory management, strengthen cash flow, and enhance profitability.

What I particularly appreciate about this book is its practical approach. It addresses real situations faced by traders every day—stock lying idle on shelves, increasing sales without corresponding profits, pressure on working capital, and the challenge of maintaining financial discipline while growing the business.

For entrepreneurs who wish to build stronger, more organized, and financially healthy businesses, this book offers valuable guidance. It encourages business owners to move beyond intuition alone and develop systems that support long-term growth.

I congratulate CA Sukanya Dilip Halyal on this initiative. I am confident that this book will serve as a useful resource for traders, distributors, retailers, and MSME entrepreneurs who aspire to build sustainable and profitable enterprises.

– Kedar Chitale

Partner

Chitale Bandhu Mithaiwale

Preface

A New Chapter for Your Business

Most merchants view their CA as someone who only handles tax returns and signatures. But over my eight years of experience, I have seen that a CA's greatest value lies in being a "Partner in Growth."

I have watched many distributors, wholesalers, and retailers struggle with the same repeating cycles of inventory pile-ups and credit traps. I realised that these entrepreneurs don't need more "accounting," but they need "clarity." They need to understand what their data is telling them so they can make better decisions every single day.

This book is my effort to put that clarity into your hands. I have simplified the "Data" of your daily operations into a roadmap you can actually use. This isn't just about book-keeping; it's about building a business that is healthy, scalable and truly profitable.

Let's move beyond the signature and start building your legacy.

Chapter 1
The Foundation

1.1 Introduction: Choosing Your Business "Vehicle"

Setting up a business is often a whirlwind of excitement. You are finding the right location for your retail outlet, scouting for the best distributors, or negotiating with wholesalers for your first big stock.

In this rush, many entrepreneurs treat the "**Legal Structure**" of their business as a mere formality—a checkbox to be ticked to get a bank account or a GST number.

This is a mistake that can cost you everything.

Choosing your business structure is like choosing the vehicle for a long journey. If you are moving goods across the street, a bicycle might work. But if you are planning to carry tonnes of cargo across the country, you need a heavy-duty truck. If you pick the wrong vehicle, you will either break down halfway or pay far more in fuel and maintenance than you ever intended.

1.2 Tale of Two Wholesalers: A Cautionary Story

To understand why this choice matters, let's look at two friends in the Garment Market: Rahul and Sanjay.

Rahul started a **traditional partnership** with his cousin. They signed a simple partnership deed and began wholesaling. Business was booming until a major fire at their warehouse, which destroyed Rs. 80 Lakhs worth of uninsured stock. Because it was a general partnership, the law saw no difference between Rahul's business and his personal life. To pay back the supplier and the bank, the court ordered the sale of Rahul's ancestral home and seized his personal savings. He did not just lose his business but also lost his family's security.

Sanjay, on the other hand, spent a little extra time and money to register as a **Private Limited Company.** When a market shift caused his distribution business to fail a few years later, the "Company" went into liquidation. While Sanjay lost the capital he invested, his personal home, his car and his wife's jewellery remained untouched. The law recognised the company as a separate legal person.

In this chapter, we will break down the four most common structures so you can choose the shield that best protects your future.

1. **The Sole Proprietorship: "One Man Show"**

   – This is the **simplest** and most common form of business for a small business owner. It is essentially an extension of yourself.

   The Pros:

   ➢ You are the boss. You don't need anyone's permission to make a decision, change your stock or pivot your strategy.

   ➢ There is no "Registration" with the Registrar of Companies. You simply get a GST number or Shop Act licence, and you are in business. It is the **cheapest** structure to start.

   ➢ Here, every bit of profit belongs to you. You don't have to share your profits with partners or shareholders.

- Usually, your Income Tax Return covers your business income. So, it has very little compliance.

The Cons:

- Here, if the business fails or gets sued, your personal assets such as your house, your car and personal bank accounts are all on the line. So here, the proprietor has "**Unlimited Liability,"** meaning that the law does not protect and distinguish your personal assets from your business.
- Banks are often hesitant to give large loans to a proprietorship compared to other business structures.
- You cannot bring investors because you cannot "Sell Shares" of yourself.
- If something happens to you, the business suffers and can effectively stop. There is no "Perpetual Succession," making it harder to pass a smooth-running business to the next generation.
- As a result, it offers **less credibility,** which can impact the growth of a business.

2. **Traditional Partnership Model:**

   – For decades, this has been the go-to for small business owners. It is basically built on trust.

   – Here, two or more people agree to share profits and losses. It is governed by the Indian Partnership Act, 1932.

The Pros:

- It is very easy to start.
- You just need a partnership deed on the stamp paper.
- There are no mandatory annual filings with the registrar.
- It is generally less expensive to create and maintain.

The Cons:

- The biggest risk is "Unlimited Liability." If the business owes money, the partners are personally liable to pay off the dues.
- Furthermore, if a partner makes a mistake or commits fraud, the other partners are legally responsible for it.

3. **Limited Liability Partnership (LLP): The Best of Both Worlds**

   – For a growing distributor or wholesaler, the LLP is often the best choice – not too heavy, not too light.

   – It's a hybrid model. It feels like a partnership, but it acts like a company.

The Pros:

- As the name suggests, the most significant advantage here is "Limited Liability," making your personal assets safe.
- Additionally, it has fewer compliance requirements as compared to a Private Limited Company.

The Cons:

- It is slightly more expensive to set up compared to a Sole Proprietorship or Partnership Firm.
- It requires mandatory annual filings and compliance with the Ministry of Corporate Affairs (MCA); failure to comply can be costly.

4. **Private Limited Company: The "Growth Engine"**

   - If your vision is to build a brand, open a chain of stores, or eventually take on investors, this is the best and only way to operate and expand.
   - It is considered a separate legal entity in the eyes of the law.
   - It can own property in its own name. It can even sue people in its own name.

The Pros:

- It gives maximum credibility as compared to any other business structure.
- Large companies and banks prefer to deal with Private Limited entities because they are seen as more "serious" and transparent.
- You can easily bring in investors by issuing shares.
- It has "Perpetual Succession," which brings businesses to live on even if the owners change or pass away.

The Cons:

- It is "Compliant heavy" under various laws, failure of which can cost heavy penalties.

- It must get its books of accounts audited by a Chartered Accountant regardless of the turnover.

1.3 Comparison of Business Structures

Factor	Proprietorship	Partnership	LLP	Pvt Ltd Company
Owners (Minimum)	1	2+	2+	2+
Liability	Unlimited	Unlimited	Limited	Limited
Legal Status	Not Separate	Not Separate	Separate Entity	Separate Entity
Compliance	Very Low	Low	Medium	High
Tax Rate	Individual Slab	30%	30%	25%/30%
Fund Raising	Difficult	Moderate	Moderate	Easy

1.4 Conclusion

Selecting the correct business is the foundation of a successful business.

The right structure helps in:

- Managing risk
- Saving taxes
- Raising finance
- Ensuring long-term stability

Before finalising the structure, business owners should consult legal and financial professionals to understand the implications.

A well-chosen structure allows the entrepreneur to focus on what matters the most, which is growing the business.

Chapter 2
The Paperwork Shield

2.1 Introduction: Applicability of Registrations for Distributors, Wholesalers and Retailers

When starting a business of trading, whether as a distributor, wholesaler, or retailer, many entrepreneurs focus primarily on purchasing goods, building supplier relationships and generating sales.

However, another equally important aspect of running a business is **obtaining the required registrations and licences from government authorities.**

These registrations serve multiple purposes:

- They make the business **legally recognised.**
- They enable the business to **operate within regulatory frameworks.**
- They help with **tax compliance.**
- They enhance **credibility** with suppliers, banks and customers.

Operating without required registrations can lead to penalties, cancellation of business operations, tax liabilities and legal consequences.

Therefore, understanding which registrations are required is essential for every trader.

2.2 Common Registrations required for Trading Business

The registrations required may vary depending on:

- Nature of business
- Turnover
- Types of products sold
- State regulations

However, most distributors and traders require the following registrations.

The list is made keeping in mind the general point of view. Some additional licences may be applicable according to the nature of the business.

Criteria	Requirement
Turnover Limit	Rs 40 Lakh for goods (Rs. 20 Lakh for special category states)
Inter-state supply	Mandatory Registration
Selling on e-commerce platforms	Mandatory
Export	Mandatory
Voluntary Registration	Allowed even below the threshold

A. **GST Registration**

- One of the most important registrations for a trading business is Goods and Services Tax (GST) Registration.
- GST applies to the supply of goods and services across India.
- When GST Registration is required:

Let us consider a few practical examples.

1. Suppose a trader in Pune starts a wholesale business of electrical accessories. Initially, his turnover may be small. However, within a year, his sales reached Rs 45 Lakh. Since his turnover exceeds the threshold limit, he must obtain GST registration. If he continues to operate without registration, he may be required to pay GST along with penalties and interest.

2. Another common situation arises in distribution businesses where traders supply goods to retailers located in different states. Even if its turnover is only Rs 15 Lakh, GST Registration becomes mandatory because **inter-state supply** requires compulsory registration under the GST Law.

   – Apart from legal compliances, GST registration offers several practical benefits. Registered businesses can claim **input tax credit,** which means that the GST paid on the purchases can be adjusted against GST collected on the sales. This reduces the overall tax burden and improves profitability.

   – Operating without GST registration when it is legally required can lead to serious consequences.

   – GST law provides for penalties, interest on unpaid tax and in certain cases even prosecution.

   – Therefore, traders should carefully evaluate whether GST registration is applicable to their business.

B. **Shop and Establishment Registration**

   – Another important registration for businesses operating from physical premises is the Shop and Establishment Registration.

- This registration is governed by state-specific laws and is generally administered by the labour department of the respective state government.
- The purpose of this law is to regulate working conditions in commercial establishments.
- For example, if a retailer opens a clothing store in a commercial market area and hires two employees to manage the shop, the business will typically be required to obtain Shop and Establishment Registration. This registration ensures that the business follows basic labour regulations and provides appropriate working conditions for employees.
- Even small retail outlets often require this registration. Many municipal authorities and banks ask for the Shop and Establishment Registration as part of documentation when opening a current bank account or applying for local business permissions.
- Failure to obtain this registration can result in penalties being imposed by labour authorities. While penalties may vary from state to state, repeated non-compliance can lead to inspections and legal action.

C. **FSSAI Licence for Food Businesses:**

- Businesses dealing in food products must obtain registration or a licence under the Food Safety and Standards Authority of India (FSSAI).
- This requirement applies to manufacturers, distributors, wholesalers, retailers and even transporters of food products.

- The objective of the FSSAI Licensing system is to ensure that food products sold to consumers meet safety and quality standards.
- For example, a wholesaler distributing packaged snacks, beverages or dairy products must obtain an FSSAI license before commencing operations. Even small grocery retailers selling packaged food items may require basic FSSAI registration.
- The level of licence depends on the size and scale of the business. Small food businesses may require basic registration, while larger distributors may require state or central licences.
- Operating a food business without FSSAI registration can lead to serious consequences. Food safety authorities have the power to impose heavy penalties, seize goods, or even shut down the business if the products are found to be unsafe or unlicensed.

D. **Drug Licence for Pharmaceutical and Cosmetic Business:**

- Businesses that deal in pharmaceutical products, medicines or certain categories of cosmetics are required to obtain a Drug Licence before starting operations.
- This licence is issued under the provisions of the Drugs and Cosmetics Act,1940 and is regulated by the State Drug Control Department.
- The primary purpose of this regulation is to ensure that medicines and regulated cosmetic products are stored, distributed and sold in a manner that protects public health.

- Medicines are sensitive products that must be handled carefully to ensure they remain safe and effective for consumers. Therefore, the government requires businesses dealing with such products to obtain proper authorisation before commencing operations.
- For distributors and wholesalers dealing in pharmaceutical products, obtaining a drug licence is mandatory. Similarly, retailers selling medicines through medical stores or pharmacies must also obtain the appropriate licence.
- In the case of cosmetics, certain regulated cosmetic products—particularly those that fall under pharmaceutical regulation—may also require licensing depending on the nature of the product and distribution channel.
- Operating a pharmaceutical or regulated cosmetic business without a valid drug licence is considered a serious offence because it may affect public health and safety.

E. **UDYAM Registration (MSME Registration)**

- UDYAM Registration is the official registration for Micro, Small and Medium Enterprises (MSMEs) in India.
- Unlike GST or FSSAI, this registration is not mandatory for most businesses, but it provides several advantages.
- Businesses registered as MSMEs gain access to various government benefits, including priority sector lending from banks, subsidies under government schemes, and protection against delayed payments from buyers.

- For example, if a distributor supplies goods to a large corporate buyer and the payment is delayed beyond the agreed credit period, the MSME law provides legal protection that allows the supplier to claim interest on delayed payments.
- Many banks also offer **easier loan approvals and lower interest rates** for MSME-registered businesses.
- Therefore, even though UDYAM registration is optional, it is highly beneficial for distributors and wholesalers seeking financial support and government incentives.

F. **Import and Export Code (IEC)**

- Businesses that intend to import goods from foreign countries or export goods outside India must obtain an Import Export Code (IEC). This code is issued by the Director General of Foreign Trade (DGFT).
- Without an IEC, a business cannot legally engage in international trade.
- For instance, suppose a trader wants to import mobile accessories from China and distribute them in the Indian market. Before importing goods, he must obtain an IEC. Similarly, if a business plans to export spices, garments, or handicrafts to international markets, IEC registration becomes mandatory.
- The registration process is relatively simple and can be completed online through the DGFT portal.

G. **PAN and Current Bank Account**

- Every business must also obtain a **Permanent Account Number (PAN)** from the Income Tax Department. PAN acts as the primary tax identification number for businesses and is required for filing income tax returns, conducting high-value financial transactions, and maintaining business records.

- Along with PAN, businesses should open a **current bank account** in the name of the business entity. Using a dedicated business bank account helps maintain proper financial records and separates personal finances from business transactions.
- Maintaining clear financial records is particularly important for traders because it supports accurate tax reporting, improves financial discipline, and builds credibility with banks and lenders.

2.3 Conclusion

- Obtaining the **appropriate registrations** is one of the most important steps when starting a distribution, wholesale or retail business.
- These registrations ensure that the business **operates legally,** gains credibility in the marketplace and remains eligible for financial and government support.
- Entrepreneurs should view registrations not as a burden but as an **essential part** of building a professional and sustainable business structure.
- By ensuring compliance from the beginning, traders can **avoid legal complications,** strengthen supplier relationships, and focus their efforts on what truly matters—growing their business and serving their customers effectively.

Chapter 3
Lack of SOPs (Standard Operating Procedures)

3.1 Introduction

Many distributors, wholesalers and retailers start their business with great enthusiasm.

They focus on purchasing goods, developing supplier relationships, and generating sales.

In the early stages, most work is handled directly by the owner. Orders are taken personally, payments are tracked manually, and inventory is managed through experience rather than systems.

While this approach may work when the business is small, problems begin to appear as the business grows. More employees are hired, more products are handled, and the number of customers increases. Without clear processes, confusion begins to arise.

- Orders may be missed.
- Inventory may not match records.
- Payments may be delayed or lost.
- Different employees may follow different methods for the same task.

This is where **Standard Operating Procedures (SOPs)** become extremely important.

SOPs help create **clarity, consistency, and control** in business operations.

3.2 What are Standard Operating Procedures (SOPs)?

A Standard Operating Procedure (SOP) is a **written set of instructions** that explains how a specific task should be performed in a business.

It ensures that everyone in the organisation performs tasks in the same way, following the same process.

SOP answers simple but critical questions:

- What needs to be done?
- Who will do it?
- How should it be done?
- When should it be done?
- In simple words, SOPs act like a **rulebook for running daily business activities.**

For example, in a trading business, there may be SOPs for:

- Receiving goods from suppliers
- Checking inventory
- Processing customer orders
- Dispatching goods
- Managing credit sales
- Collecting payments

When these procedures are clearly defined, the business operates smoothly even when the owner is not present.

3.3 Why SOPs Are Important?

SOPs play a crucial role in building a stable and scalable business. Without SOPs, businesses often depend entirely on the owner's presence and personal supervision.

As the business grows, it becomes difficult for one person to control every activity. SOPs help distribute responsibilities while maintaining control over operations.

The importance of SOPs can be understood through the following aspects.

Benefit	Explanation
Consistency	Every employee follows the same process
Efficiency	Tasks are completed faster and more accurately
Reduced errors	Clear instructions reduce mistakes
Training support	New employees can learn quickly
Business scalability	Business can grow without operational chaos
Accountability	Responsibilities are clearly defined

In essence, SOPs help convert a **person-dependent business into a system-driven business**.

3.4 SOPs in a Trading Business

Distributors, Wholesalers, and Retailers deal with several operational activities daily.

If these activities are not standardised, it can create confusion and financial loss.

Some of the key areas where SOPs are essential include:

Business Area	SOP Requirement
Purchase Management	How to place orders with suppliers
Inventory Management	How to record stock movement
Order processing	Steps for receiving and confirming orders
Dispatch Management	Packing and shipping procedures
Credit Sales	Approval and Monitoring of customer credit
Payment Collection	Process for follow-up and reconciliation
Returns Management	Handling damaged or returned goods

Each of these activities directly affects the profitability and efficiency of the business.

3.5 Business Story: The Missing Inventory Problem

Consider the story of Mr. Amit, who runs a distribution business for electrical goods. His business was growing rapidly. He had five employees managing the warehouse and dispatch operations. However, he never created clear procedures for stock management.

Each employee followed their own method for storing goods and recording dispatches.

After a few months, Mr. Amit noticed a serious problem. The inventory records showed 500 units of a particular product, but the warehouse only had 380 units.

After the investigation, he discovered several issues:

- Goods were dispatched without proper entry.
- Returns from customers were not recorded.
- Damaged items were not documented.

The absence of SOPs resulted in inventory losses and confusion among employees.

Mr. Amit eventually introduced SOPs for inventory management, dispatch and returns. Within a few months, stock discrepancies were significantly reduced.

This example clearly shows how SOPs protect businesses from operational losses.

3.6 Consequences of Not Having SOPs

Businesses that operate without SOPs often face several operational and financial challenges.

First, employees may perform tasks differently, leading to **inconsistency in operations.**

Second, mistakes become more frequent because there are **no clear instructions or accountability.**

Third, the business becomes heavily dependent on the owner's personal supervision. If the owner is absent, operations may slow down or become disorganised.

The following table highlights common consequences of the absence of SOPs.

Problem	Impact on Business
Inventory mismatch	Financial Losses
Order errors	Customer dissatisfaction
Payment tracking issues	Cash flow problems
Employee confusion	Reduced productivity
Fraud Risk	Lack of internal control

Over time, these problems can significantly affect the profitability and reputation of the business.

3.7 Consequences of Not Following SOPs

Even when SOPs exist, they must be **properly implemented** and followed.

If employees ignore established procedures, the benefits of SOPs are lost.

For example, a distributor may have an SOP requiring stock verification before dispatch.

However, if employees skip this step during busy periods, wrong quantities may be delivered to customers.

This can result in

- Customer complaints.
- Additional logistical costs.
- Loss of business credibility.

Therefore, SOPs must not only be created but also **regularly monitored and enforced**.

3.8 How SOPs Help Businesses Grow

As businesses expand, the complexity of operations increases. SOPs play a crucial role in enabling growth.

When processes are standardised:

- New employees can be trained quickly
- Work can be delegated with confidence
- Operational errors are minimised
- Business owners can focus on strategic decisions rather than daily supervision

Many successful distribution companies rely heavily on SOPs to manage large operations efficiently.

3.9 Conclusion

Standard Operating Procedures are an **essential part** of building a professional and scalable trading business.

For distributors, wholesalers, and retailers, SOPs help create **clarity in operations, improve efficiency, and reduce operational risks.**

Businesses that rely solely on informal practices often struggle with inventory issues, payment delays, and operational confusion. On the other hand, businesses that implement clear SOPs are better equipped to manage growth and maintain control over their operations.

Entrepreneurs should therefore invest time in developing and implementing SOPs for all critical business activities.

A well-designed SOP system transforms a business from being **person-dependent to system-driven**, which is a key step toward long-term success.

Chapter 4
Ignoring Books of Accounts

4.1 Introduction

In many trading businesses—especially among distributors, wholesalers and retailers, it is very common to see that proper books of accounts are either not maintained at all or are maintained only for name's sake.

Business owners often believe that:

- I know my business, I don't need records.
- As long as money is coming, everything is fine.
- Accounts can be managed at year-end for tax purposes.

While this approach may work temporarily, it creates serious financial and compliance risks in the long run.

Maintaining proper books of accounts is not just an accounting requirement—**it is a basic foundation for running a financially healthy business.**

4.2 What are Books of Accounts?

Books of Accounts refer to a systematic record of all financial transactions of a business.

These include:

- Sales records
- Purchase records
- Cash transactions
- Bank transactions
- Sundry Debtors (amount receivable from customers)
- Sundry Creditors (amount payable to suppliers)
- Expenses and Income

In simple terms, books of accounts answer three very important questions:

- How much are you earning?
- How much are you spending?
- How much money is available?

Without proper records, a business owner is essentially operating **without knowing the true financial position of the business.**

4.3 Why Traders Ignore Book-Keeping

In practical scenarios, many traders ignore book-keeping due to the following reasons:

- Lack of accounting knowledge
- Dependence on memory or informal records
- Focus on daily operations rather than financial control
- Belief that accounting is only required for tax filing

For example, a retailer may maintain only a rough notebook for daily sales and expenses. A distributor may rely on WhatsApp messages or informal communication for tracking orders and payments.

While such practices may seem convenient, they create **major financial blind spots**.

4.4 Legal Requirement to Maintain Books of Accounts

Maintaining books of accounts is not just a good practice—it is also mandatory under law in certain cases.

Under the Income Tax Law,

As per the Income Tax Law, certain businesses are required to maintain books of accounts if:

- Income exceeds prescribed limits
- Turnover crosses specified thresholds
- Business is not covered under presumptive taxation, or opts out of it

Under the GST Law

Businesses registered under GST are required to maintain records such as:

- Sales register
- Purchase register
- Stock records
- Input Tax Credit records

Failure to maintain proper records can lead to **penalties and assessments based on estimation**.

4.5 Practical Example: The Illusion of Profit

Let us consider a real-life situation.

Mr. Ramesh runs a wholesale business in plastic goods. He has good sales and regular customers. He believes his business is profitable because:

- Sales are increasing
- Cash Flow is continuous

However, he does not maintain proper books of accounts.

At the end of the year, when accounts are prepared, the reality is different:

- A large amount is stuck in debtors (customers have not paid)
- Excess stock is lying unsold
- Expenses were higher than expected

The business was making very low profit, but Mr. Ramesh assumed it was doing well.

This situation is very common in trading businesses where profit is confused with Cash Flow.

4.6 Importance of Maintaining Proper Books

Maintaining proper books of accounts helps business owners in multiple ways.

First, it provides financial clarity. The owner knows exactly how much profit is being earned and where money is being spent.

Second, it helps in decision-making. For example:

- Which product is profitable?
- Which customer is delaying payments?
- Where can expenses be reduced?

Third, it improves Cash Flow management. By tracking receivables and payables, the business can ensure smooth operations without financial stress.

Fourth, it builds credibility with banks and lenders. Proper financial records are essential for obtaining loans and credit facilities.

Finally, it ensures **legal compliance**, avoiding penalties and disputes with tax authorities.

4.7 Key Books Every Trader Should Maintain

While accounting systems can be detailed, every trader should at least maintain basic records.

Book/Record	Purpose
Sales Register	Track all sales transactions
Purchase Register	Track all purchase transactions
Cash Book	Record daily cash transactions
Bank Book	Track bank transactions
Debtors Ledger	Track customer outstandings
Creditors Ledger	Track supplier dues
Stock Register	Track inventory movements

Even simple accounting software or Excel can be used to maintain these records effectively.

4.8 Consequences of Not Maintaining Books

Ignoring books of accounts can lead to serious consequences, both financially and legally.

Financial Consequences:

When proper records are not maintained

- Profit cannot be accurately determined
- Cash shortages go unnoticed
- Inventory losses are not tracked
- Receivables and Payables become weak

This leads to **financial leakage and reduced profitability.**

Legal Consequences:

From a compliance perspective, failure to maintain books of accounts can result in:

- Income Tax Penalties for non-maintenance of books of accounts
- GST Penalties for improper record keeping
- Disallowance of expenses if they are not supported by records
- At the time of assessment, income may be estimated by the authorities

Practical Example: Tax Notice Situation

A trader receives a notice from the Income Tax Department asking for details of income and expenses.

However, due to a lack of proper books:

- He cannot justify the expenses.
- He cannot explain cash deposits.
- He cannot reconcile the turnover.

As a result, the Tax Officer may estimate income at a higher level, leading to higher tax liability and penalties.

4.9 Consequences of Improper Book-keeping

Even if books are maintained, but not properly, similar problems arise.

For example:

- Sales are recorded but not matched with GST Returns
- Purchases recorded without proper invoices
- Cash transactions are not reconciled

This creates discrepancies that can lead to:

- GST Notices
- Mismatch in returns
- Financial misstatement

Therefore, maintaining books is not enough; they must be accurate and regularly updated.

4.10 How Proper Books Help Business Growth

Maintaining proper books of accounts transforms the way a business operates.

It allows the owner to:

- Monitor profitability in real time
- Control expenses effectively
- Identify Slow-Moving Stock
- Manage Working Capital effectively
- Plan for expansion

Many successful distributors and wholesalers rely heavily on the financial data to make business decisions.

A business with proper accounts is always in a better position to grow compared to one operating without financial clarity.

4.11 Conclusion

Books of accounts are not just a compliance requirement, but they are a powerful tool for business success.

Ignoring book-keeping may seem convenient in short term, but it leads to confusion, financial losses and legal risks. On the other hand, maintaining proper books provides clarity, control, and confidence to the business owner.

A business that knows its numbers is always in a stronger position to survive, grow and succeed.

Chapter 5
Mastering Working Capital

5.1 Introduction

In the world of trading, there is a famous saying: "**Profit is a concept, but Cash is reality**"

You might have a shop full of premium stock and a ledger showing lakhs of rupees in sales, but if you don't have enough cash in the bank to pay your electricity bill or your staff's salary tomorrow, your business is in trouble. This "Ready-to-Use" money is what we call **Working Capital.**

Think of Working Capital as the Fuel in your delivery truck. You can have the best truck (your business structure) and a clear destination (your goals), but without fuel, you are not going anywhere.

For a trader, managing working capital is the art of ensuring that cash flows into the business faster than it flows out. It is the difference between a business that runs smoothly and one that is constantly on the verge of collapse.

5.2 A Story of the "Rich Merchant"

Imagine two distributors in the same city, Ramesh and Suresh. Both sell electrical goods.

Ramesh believes in "Big Volume." He buys massive amounts of stock to get the best discounts from manufacturers. His warehouse is overflowing. To sell this stock quickly, he gives his customers 90 days to pay. On paper, Ramesh is a "Big Man."

Suresh is different. He buys only what he can sell in 15 days. He is strict with his customers; they must pay him within 21 days, or he stops the next delivery.

When a sudden market opportunity arrived, a new smart-lighting range that everyone wanted. Suresh had cash ready to grab the opportunity. Ramesh, however, had all his money "stuck" in the stock in his warehouse and in the pockets of customers who had not paid him yet.

Ramesh was "Asset Rich," but he could not pay his electricity bill. Suresh had "Working Capital" ready in his hand, and therefore, he stayed ahead in the game.

5.3 Understanding the Trading Cycle: A "Cash to Cash" Journey

To understand working capital, you must look at your business not as a series of sales but as a continuous circle. This is known as the **Operating Cycle.**

For a Trader, money moves in a circle. The faster this circle spins, the wealthier you become.

1. **CASH:** You start with your initial capital.
2. **STOCK:** You use that cash to buy goods from manufacturers or wholesalers. At this moment, your "Liquid Cash" turns into "Physical Boxes"
3. **SALES:** You sell those goods to a customer.

4. **RECEIVABLES:** If you sell on credit, your money is now stuck in your customer's pocket. It is an entry in your book as a receivable.

5. **COLLECTION:** Finally, the customer pays you, and the money returns to your bank account, ready to start the cycle again.

The Working Capital Gap: This is the time between Step 1 (Paying your supplier) and Step 5 (Getting paid by your customer). Your job as a smart merchant is to make this gap as small as possible.

The Golden Rule of Trading: The faster this cycle spins, the less "extra" money you need to pump into the business. If your cycle takes 90 days to complete, your money is only working for you four times a year. If you can shorten it to 30 days, that same money works for you 12 times a year, effectively tripling your business potential without adding a single rupee of new capital.

5.4 Three Pillars for Effective Working Capital Management:

Pillar 1: Inventory Management: Avoiding "Sleeping Cash"

In trading, your warehouse is where your money goes to sleep. Every box sitting on a shelf is "frozen cash" that you cannot use to pay rent, salaries or electricity.

- **The Overstocking Trap:** Suppliers often offer "schemes" like "Buy 500 units to get a 5% discount." While it looks like saving, you must calculate the **Carrying Cost**. If these 500 units take six months to sell, the interest you pay on the money borrowed to buy them will likely be much higher than the 5% discount you received.

- **The Danger of Dead Stock:** Goods that haven't moved in 60 to 90 days are "Dead Stock." They are like a leak in a water tank. They take up expensive warehouse space and lose value over a period. Smart merchants audit their stock monthly and "flush out" slow-moving items, even at cost price, to bring the cash back into the cycle.
- **The 80-20 Rule:** In almost every trading business, 80% of the profit comes from 20% of the products. Focus your working capital on these "Fast Movers." Don't let your cash get tied up in "prestige items" that look good on the shelf but rarely sell.

Pillar 2: Trade Receivables: Managing the "Udhaari"

In the Indian trade market, credit is often a necessity. However, a merchant must remember: **you are a trader, not a bank.**

When you give a customer 60 days to pay, you are essentially giving them an interest-free loan.

- **The Cost of Waiting:** If you borrow from a bank at 12% interest to run your shop, every day a customer delays the payment costs you money. If a customer takes three months to pay, you have effectively lost 3% of your profit margin just in interest costs.
- **Strict Credit Limits:** Every customer must have a "ceiling." If a customer has not cleared their previous bill, the next shipment should be paused. It is better to lose a sale than to lose the cost of the goods entirely.
- **Power of Cash Discounts:** Offering 1% or 2% discount for immediate payment is often much cheaper than the cost of chasing a customer for months. It improves your "Cash Flow" and reduces the risk of bad debts.

Pillar 3: Trade Payables—Using Supplier Credit Strategically

Your suppliers are your biggest source of interest-free funding. Managing how you pay them is just as important as how you collect from customers.

- **The Ideal Balance:** The secret to a "Smooth Business" is ensuring **"your Collection Period is shorter than your Payment Period."** If you collect money from customers in 20 days but pay your suppliers in 30 days, you are using the supplier's money to run your operations.

- **Reputation as Capital:** A merchant who pays on time is a merchant who gets the first call when there is a hot new product or a special price drop. Your "Credit Worthiness" with suppliers is as valuable as cash in the bank.

5.5 The Deadly Consequences of Poor Working Capital Management

When a merchant ignores the flow of working capital, the business enters a "Death Spiral." Even if the shop is busy, the following problems will arise:

- **The Interest Trap**: When cash runs out, merchants turn to high-interest market loans or bank overdrafts. Eventually, the interest payments become so high that they eat up the entire profit margin. You end up working for the lender, not yourself.

- **Losing Supplier Support:** If you delay payments, suppliers will stop giving you priority. You will be left with slow-moving stock or poor-quality goods because the "hot" items are being sent to competitors who pay on time.

- **The "Desperation Sale":** When you need cash urgently to pay salaries or GST, you are forced to sell stock at a loss or a massive discount. This "firefighting" destroys the long-term health of the business.
- **Operational Paralysis:** You spend 90% of your time worrying about "where the money will come from" instead of focusing on "how to grow the sales." Growth stops when the owner is constantly stressed about daily payments.
- **Missed Growth Opportunities:** Opportunities do not wait for your customers to pay you. If a prime shop location or a lucrative new distributorship opens, you won't have the "Liquid Cash" to grab it.

5.6 Practical Strategies for a Smooth Flow:

To ensure your business stays healthy and runs without friction, follow these practical steps:

- **Maintain a Cash Buffer:** Always keep a "Reserve Fund" equal to at least one month of operating expenses. This ensures you never have to take a **high-interest emergency loan** for basic needs like rent or electricity.
- **Weekly Ageing Reports:** Once a week, look at your "Debtors List." Identify who is crossing the 30-day or 45-day mark. These should be your first phone calls at the start of the week.
- **Separate Personal from Business:** Never treat the "Galla" (Cash Drawer) as a personal ATM. Taking money out for personal expenses without recording it makes it impossible to know your true working capital position.

- **The "One-In, One-Out" Rule:** For every new line of stock you bring in, try to clear out an old, slow-moving line. This keeps your warehouse lean and your cash moving.

5.7 Conclusion

In the world of trade, profit is a matter of opinion, but cash is a matter of fact. A business can survive a year of low profit, but it cannot survive a week of zero cash flow.

Managing your working capital is not about being "stingy"; it is about being disciplined. By keeping your inventory lean, your collections fast, and your payments strategic, you create a "Seamless Business." When your finances are under control, your business stops being a source of stress and starts being the engine of your success.

Always Remember: DON'T JUST CHASE THE SALE, CHASE THE CASH.

Chapter 6
Cash Flow: The Oxygen of Your Business

6.1 Introduction

In the previous chapter, we discussed about Working Capital—the Engine of your business. Now, we must talk about the fuel that keeps the engine running: **Cash Flow**

There is a dangerous trap that many merchants fall into. They look at their sales at the end of the month, see a healthy margin, and assume their business is doing great. But then Monday morning arrives, and they don't have enough money in the bank to pay the GST or the warehouse rent.

This happens because of a simple truth: **Profit is not the same as Cash.**

Profit is an accounting concept. It is what you expect to have after all your sales are done and expenses are recorded. **Cash is what you have in your hand** right now. A business can survive for years without making a profit (by burning through capital or loans), but it cannot survive for a single day without cash. Cash is the oxygen of your business. If the flow stops, the business suffocates.

6.2 The Story of Sanjay: The "Successful" Wholesaler Who Almost Collapsed

Sanjay ran a thriving wholesale business selling kitchen appliances. In the month of October, he landed a massive order from a large retail chain for the festive season. He sold Rs 50 Lakh worth of goods with a 20% profit margin. On paper, Sanjay had just made Rs 10 Lakhs in profit. He was thrilled.

However, the retail chain had a policy of paying after 90 days.

Meanwhile, Sanjay had to pay his manufacturers for the stock within 15 days to keep his "Preferred Dealer" status. He also had to pay his ten employees their festive bonuses, cover increased transport costs and pay his own household expenses.

By November, Sanjay was in a panic. Even though he was "profitable" by Rs 10 Lakhs, his bank account was not showing enough balance. He had plenty of profit on his ledger, but not enough "**Cash Flow"** to run his life. To pay his staff, he ended up taking a "Market Loan" at a staggering 3% interest per month. By the time the retail chain finally paid him in January, nearly half of his Rs 10 Lakh profit had been swallowed by interest payments.

The Lesson: Sanjay focused on the Sale, but he forgot to manage the Flow. He learned the hard way that you cannot pay your staff with "expected profit."

6.3 The Deep Dive: Why Profit is NOT EQUAL to Cash

As a merchant, you must understand three reasons why your profit does not match your bank balance:

- **The Inventory Weight:** When you buy Rs 10 Lakhs of stocks, your profits do not change, but your cash drops by Rs 10 Lakhs immediately. That money is now frozen in boxes.

- **The Credit Gap (Receivables):** When you sell that stock for Rs 12 Lakhs on credit, your profit shows Rs 2 Lakhs earned. But your cash has not increased by a single rupee yet.
- **Asset Purchase:** If you buy a new delivery van for Rs 8 Lakhs, it does not show up as an "expense" in your monthly profit report (only a small part called depreciation does). But Rs 8 Lakh of real cash has left your bank account instantly.

6.4 The Two Streams: CASH INFLOW vs. CASH OUTFLOW

To manage your cash flow, visualise your business as a water tank.

Cash Inflow (The Tap)

This is the monthly flowing into your Tank. For a Trader, this comes from

- **Cash Sales:** The best kind of inflow, which is immediate and certain.
- **Collections from Credit Customers:** Money arriving from past sales.
- **Other Income:** Selling scrap packaging, old furniture or receiving a tax refund.

Cash Outflow (The Drain)

This is the money flowing out of your tank. For a Trader, this includes:

- **Stock Purchases:** Paying your suppliers and distributors.
- **Operating Expenses:** Paying Rent, Salaries, Electricity, and Transport.
- **Taxes and Interest:** Paying GST, Income Tax and Interest on Bank Cash Credit (CC) limits.
- **Personal Drawings:** The money you take out for your household expenses.

The Goal: You must ensure that the "Tap" (Inflow) stays open enough to keep the tank full, even while the "Drain" (Outflow) is constantly taking money away.

6.5 Master the "Cash Flow Forecast"

You don't need complex accounting software for this. You only need a simple 4-week calendar. At the start of every month, look ahead and map out your "Cash Journey"

- **The "Must-Pays" (Fixed Dates):** Mark the fixed expenses like Rental, Salaries and GST Expenses. These are your non-negotiable outflows.
- **The "Expected Collections":** Based on your credit terms, who is scheduled to pay you this week? Be realistic. If a customer always pays 10 days late, mark them down for the later date.
- **The "Big Buys":** When are you planning to restock?

Why do this?

If you see that in week 3, you have a GST payment of Rs 2 Lakhs and a supplier payment of Rs 3 lakhs, but your expected collections are only Rs 1 lakh, you have a **Cash Flow Gap** of Rs 4 lakhs.

The Solution: Because you saw these 20 days in advance, you can:

1. Call your top five customers and offer a 1% "Special Early Payment Discount."
2. Ask your supplier if you can pay in two instalments.
3. Delay a non-essential purchase (like new office furniture).

6.6 Managing the "Cash Credit" (CC) Limit.

Most wholesalers use a Bank CC (Cash Credit) or Overdraft limit. While this is a great tool, it can be a "slow poison" if misused.

- **The Right Way:** Use the CC limit to cover the 15–20-day gap between paying the supplier and receiving money from a customer.
- **The Wrong Way:** Using the CC limit to buy "Dead Stock" or for personal expenses. If your CC limit is always "maxed out," it means your cash flow is broken. You are no longer running the business, but the interest is running you.

6.7 Strategic Moves for Healthy Cash Flow

1. **1. Speed up the inflow**
    - **Partial Advance:** For large orders, ask for 20% advance. This covers your transport and immediate costs.
    - **Invoice Discipline:** Don't wait until the weekend to raise the bills. Invoice the moment the goods leave your warehouse. A three-day delay in invoicing is a three-day delay in getting paid.

2. **Slow down the outflow**

   - **Staggered Payments:** Instead of paying all your utility bills on the same day, spread them out if possible.
   - **Inventory Discipline:** Don't be a "Stock Hoarder." Every extra box is cash that could have been in your bank, earning interest or paying a bill.

3. **The "Safety Buffer":** Aim to keep a "Cash Reserve" "Cash Reserve" equal to three months of your fixed operating expenses. (Rent + Salaries) This protects you during a market strike, a pandemic, or a sudden drop in demand.

6.8 Conclusion: Control the Flow, Build the Success.

Profit tells you how smart you are at buying and selling. But Cash Flow tells you how long you will stay in the business.

As a merchant, your focus should always be on "Liquidity." A "Liquid" business has cash ready for opportunities and emergencies. When you manage your cash flow effectively, you stop being a servant to your bills and start being the master of your growth.

The Merchant's Mantra:

Sales are a Vanity (for show)

Profit is a Sanity (for the mind)

But Cash is the Reality (for survival)

Chapter 7

Inventory–Wealth on your Shelves or a Hole in Your Pocket?

7.1 Introduction

As a Wholesaler or Distributor, your business revolves around one thing: **INVENTORY.**

In your warehouse, you don't see boxes of electronics, garments, or hardware—you should see piles of currency notes sitting on those shelves.

The biggest mistake a merchant can make is treating inventory as "stuff" rather than "cash." If you dropped a Rs. 2,000 note on the warehouse floor, you would pick it up immediately. But many traders allow thousands of rupees worth of inventory to get damaged, lost, or expire without a second thought.

Mishandling inventory is the fastest way to drain your bank account. In this chapter, we will look at how inventory is mismanaged, the heavy price you pay for it and how to build a system that protects your wealth.

7.2 The Story of Manish: The "Scheme" Collector

Manish was a successful distributor of FMCG goods. He had a simple philosophy: "More inventory means more sales." Whenever a company offered a "10+1" scheme or a 5% bulk discount, Manish jumped on it. He filled his warehouse to the ceiling.

However, Manish didn't have a system. New inventory was always pushed to the front, while the old inventory was pushed to the dark corners of the warehouse.

One day, Manish decided to clean the back of his warehouse. He found fifty cases of biscuits that had expired six months ago. He found 20 crates of expensive soap that had been chewed by rats. He also realised he had enough shampoo to last him three years, while he was "out of inventory" of the fast-moving toothpaste his customers actually wanted.

Manish thought he was getting "discounts," but in reality, his "savings" were rotting in the dark. He had a warehouse full of products, but no cash to pay his electricity bill.

7.3 How Inventory is Mishandled: The Common Mistakes

Inventory mismanagement does not happen overnight; it happens through small, daily errors:

- **The Over-Buying Trap:** Buying purely based on supplier discounts rather than customer demand. This leads to "Dead Inventory" that never moves.
- **The "LIFO" Mistake (Last in First Out):** When new inventory arrives, workers often place it in front of the

old inventory because it's easier. The old inventory stays at the back until it expires or becomes obsolete.

- **Poor Storage Conditions:** Storing sensitive goods near moisture, heat or directly on the floor. Rats, dampness and dust can destroy thousands of rupees in a single night.
- **The "Invisible" Inventory:** Not knowing exactly what you have can create problems. If you don't know you have 10 units in the back, you might order 10 more units, doubling your blocked capital.
- **Shrinkage (Theft and Leakage):** Without a tracking system, small items "disappear." Whether it is employee theft or unrecorded samples given to customers, these small leaks add up to a massive hole in your profit.

7.4 The Consequences of Poor Inventory Management

If you don't control your inventory, it will eventually control you. Here is the price you pay:

- **Frozen Capital:** Your money is "Stuck." You can't use it to pay bills, buy new trending products, or expand your shop because it is tied up in slow-moving boxes.
- **High Carrying Costs:** You pay for a larger warehouse than you need, extra insurance, more electricity for cooling and more staff to manage "junk" inventory.
- **The "Out of Box" Paradox:** Ironically, merchants with too much inventory are often out of the right inventory. When a customer asks for a fast-moving item, and you don't have it, they go to your competitor. You lose the sale and the customer.

- **Forced Discounts:** When inventory gets old or near expiry, you are forced to sell it at a loss just to get rid of it.

- **Tax and Audit Hassles:** During year-end, if your physical inventory does not match your books, you face legal and tax complications. The government expects you to pay tax on what you should have had.

7.5 The "Ideal Inventory System" for the Modern Merchant

You don't need a million-dollar software to manage inventory. You need discipline. An ideal system follows these five steps:

A. **The ABC Analysis (The "Smart" Focus)**

Not all inventory is equal. Divide your inventory into three categories.

- **Category A:** Fast-moving items that bring in 70% of your revenue. Track these **daily.** Never let these run out.

- **Category B:** Moderate movers. Track these **weekly.**

- **Category C:** Slow-moving or "Fancy" items. Track these **monthly.** Don't overinvest here.

B. **The FIFO Rule (First-In, First-Out)**

This is the golden rule of trading. The oldest inventory must always be sold first.

- **Practical Tip:** Train your staff to load new inventory at the back or bottom of the pile. Label every batch with a "Date of Arrival" stick in large, bold letters.

C. **The "Physical vs Digital" Match**

At least once a month, do a "Cycle Count." Choose five random items and count them physically. Does the number on the shelf match the number in your notebook or computer? If not, find out why immediately.

D. **The Re-Order Level (The Red Line)**

For every product, decide on a "Danger Mark." For example, if you have only 10 cases of Oil left, you must order more today." This prevents "Out-of-Inventory" situations and stops you from placing panic orders at high prices.

E. **Proper Positioning and Labelling**

Every item should have a "home." Don't just dump boxes. Use racks, pallets and clear labels. If you can't find an item within a minute, your warehouse is mismanaged.

7.6 Conclusion: Clean Warehouse, Clear Mind

Managing inventory is like managing your health. If you eat too much (overbuy) and don't move (slow sales), the business becomes sluggish and diseased.

A clean, organised warehouse where every box is accounted for is a sign of a profitable business. When you control your inventory, you control your cash. And when you control your cash, "Success" is no longer a matter of luck—it becomes a certainty.

The Merchant's Rule"

If you haven't touched a box in 90 days, it's no longer an asset, but it's a liability. Sell it, clear the space and get your cash back.

Chapter 8
The Tug-of-War - Balancing What You Owe vs. What You Are Owed

8.1 Introduction

Managing Receivables and Payables Are Two Sides of the Same Coin.

In the daily life of a wholesaler or distributor, every morning begins with two lists:

- List A: The people who owe you money (**Receivables** or Debtors)
- List B: The people you owe money to (**Payables** or Creditors)

Running a successful trading business is like a perpetual tug-of-war between these two lists. If List A (Receivables) grows too large and heavy, your business collapses because you have no cash. If List B (Payables) is neglected, your reputation in the market is ruined, and suppliers will stop sending you goods.

Most merchants fail not because they don't have customers, but because they lose control of this balance. They focus so much on selling that they are effectively running a "mini bank" in the middle of their warehouse. This chapter will show you how to manage both sides, so your business stays upright and profitable.

8.2 The Merchant's Mirror: A Story of the "Perfect Balance"

Consider the case of two wholesalers in the textile market, Suresh and Ramesh, who have their own shops.

Suresh believed that "Sales are Everything." To grow quickly, he gave his customers 60 days to pay. However, his suppliers only gave him 15 days to pay. Every month, he faced a "30- Days Gap" where he had to find lakhs of rupees to pay his suppliers while waiting for his customers. He was constantly stressed, taking high-interest loans, and eventually, his interest costs ate up his entire profit.

Ramesh understood the "Balance." He negotiated with his supplier for 30 days of credit. At the same time, he told his customers that they must pay within 21 days. Because he collected money in 21 days and paid his suppliers in 30 days, he always had a "9 Days Buffer" where the supplier's money was sitting in his bank account.

He did not just sell cloth; he managed the **Timing of Money.** Suresh was working for a bank, while Ramesh made the money work for him.

8.3 Managing Receivables" Protecting Your "Udhaari"

While you give a customer credit, you are essentially lending them your hard-earned money for free. You must treat your receivables with the same respect you treat the cash in your drawer.

The "Ladder of Collection"

Don't wait for a bill to become "Overdue" before you act. Use this three-step ladder:

Step 1: The Soft Reminder (7 Days Before Due Date): Send a polite automated message or a quick WhatsApp. This ensures they don't forget.

Step 2: The Action Call (On Due Date): If the payment hasn't arrived, a phone call is mandatory. Ask for the specific time and mode of payment.

Step 3: The Stop-Supply Rule (1 Day Past Due): This is the most important rule. If a customer hasn't cleared their old bill, do not send a single new box of stock. If you keep supplying to a customer who doesn't pay on time, you aren't a trader; you are a donor.

Know Your "Bad Apples"

Every market has customers who are "Professional Delayers." They pay everyone else but wait for you to beg. **Flag them.** Limit their credit to a very small amount or move them to a "Cash Only" or "100% Advance" basis. Your time is better spent finding a new customer who pays on time than chasing an old one who doesn't.

8.4 Managing Payables: Protecting Your Reputation

Your "Payables" list is not just a debt; it is your Reputation. "Payables" list is not just a debt; it is your **Reputation.** In the wholesale world, your word is your bond.

The "Early Payment" Strategy

Suppliers love merchants who pay early. Sometimes, paying a supplier 5 days early can get you an extra 1% or 2% "Cash Discount." Over a year, these small discounts add up to a massive increase in your net profit.

Communication is Currency

If you are facing a genuine cash crunch and cannot pay a supplier on the due date, **do not switch off your phone.**

- Call them before the due date.
- Explain the situation honestly.
- Tell them exactly when they will receive the money (even if it's in two instalments).

Suppliers will respect your honesty and continue to support you. They only get angry when you disappear.

8.5 The Golden Ratio: The 7 Day Rule

As a simple guide for a merchant, try to follow the **7-Day Rule:**

Always aim to collect your money at least 7 days BEFORE you must pay your suppliers.

If you achieve this, you will never have to visit a moneylender or worry about bank interest. You are using the "Market's Money" to grow your own empire.

8.6 Consequences of Mishandling the Balance

If the tug-of-war goes wrong, the consequences can be severe:

1. **The Liquidity Trap:** You have crores in sales but can't pay your child's school fees or your own house EMI/Rent.
2. **Supplier Blacklisting:** Once the word spreads that you are a "slow payer," big brands will stop giving you their distributorship.

3. **The Interest Death-Spiral:** You take a loan to pay a supplier because a customer didn't pay you. Now, you must collect even more from the customer just to cover the bank's interest.

8.7 Conclusion: The Healthy Heartbeat of Trade

Managing receivables and payables is the "heartbeat" of your shop. When the heart beats at the right rhythm, collecting fast and paying strategically, the whole business stays healthy.

Remember:

- A Sale is a **GIFT** until you collect the money.
- A Debt is a **BURDEN** until you pay the supplier.

Keep your collections tight, your payments honest, and your "Gap" small. That is the secret to a stress-free and successful trading life.

Chapter 9

The Loan Game: Master the Debt, or It Will Master You

9.1 Introduction: The Double-Edged Sword

In the world of trade, a loan is like a sharp sword. In the hands of a skilled warrior, it can conquer new territories and grow an empire. In the hands of someone careless, it can cause a deep, self-inflicted wound.

Many merchants believe that "taking a loan is a sign of a big business." This is a dangerous myth. A loan is simply a tool.

It is "rented money." Just as you pay rent for your warehouse, you pay interest to "rented" capital.

If that rented capital does not help you make more profit than the cost of the rent, you are moving backward, not forward.

In this chapter, we will explore how to play the "Loan Game" so that you stay in control and don't end up working as an unpaid employee for the bank.

9.2 The Tale of Two Traders: Scale vs. Survival

To understand the strategy, let's look at two neighbours in the wholesale market, Ajay and Vijay.

Ajay took a Cash Credit (CC) Limit of Rs. 20 Lakhs. He used it strategically. When a major supplier offered a "Pre-season Discount" of 8% for a bulk cash purchase, Ajay used his CC limit to buy the stock. He sold the entire stock in 45 days.

Even after paying the bank 1.5% interest for those two months, he still made an extra 6.5% profit that his competitors couldn't get.

Ajay used the loan for growth.

Vijay also had a Cash Credit (CC) of Rs 20 Lakh. But Vijay used it differently. He used it to pay his old electricity bills, his staff salaries, and his personal home EMI because his customers weren't paying him on time. The interest kept ticking every month, but Vijay wasn't using the money to generate new sales. He was simply using "tomorrow's money" to pay for "yesterday's mistakes."

Vijay used the loan for Survival.

Ajay's business expanded; Vijay's business was eventually swallowed by the Bank's Interest.

9.3 The Merchant's Menu: Types of Loans

As a Trader, you don't need every type of loan. You need to pick the right "vehicle" for your specific need.

1. **Cash Credit (CC)/Overdraft (OD):** This is the most common "Running Loan" for traders. You only pay interest on the amount you actually use. It's like a flexible tap. You can open it when you need to buy stock and close it (by depositing cash) when your customers pay you.

2. **Term Loans:** These are for the "Big Bones" of your business. Use these only if you are buying a shop, a warehouse or

a delivery truck. These are paid back in fixed monthly instalments (EMIs) over three to five years.

3. **Unsecured Business Loans:** These are quick but expensive. Banks give these based on your GST returns or ITR.

   Warning: The interest rates here are much higher. Use these only for very short-term emergencies, never for long-term expansions.

4. **Market/Private Loans:** Borrowing from local money lenders at 2% or 3% per month. This is the "Emergency Room" of finance. If you stay here too long, your business will die.

9.4 Strategic Rules of the Game

Before you sign a loan document, ask yourself these three "CA-Approved" Questions:

1. **The Margin Test:** Is the profit I will make from this money significantly higher than the interest I am paying? If you pay 12% interest to make a 10% margin, you are losing 2% every year just by staying in the business.
2. **The "Purpose" Test:** Am I using this for an **Asset** (something that makes money, like stock) or a **Liability** (something that costs money, like a fancy office Interior)?
3. **The Repayment Reality**: If my biggest customer delays payment by 60 days, do I have enough "own cash" to pay the bank's interest? If the answer is no, the loan is too big for you.

9.5 The Silent Partner: How Interest Eats Your Profit

When you take a loan, the bank becomes your **"Silent Partner."** Unlike a real partner, the bank doesn't care if you had a bad sales month, if a fire broke out, or if you were sick. The bank wants its "share" (interest) every single month.

Imagine your business makes a 15% net profit. If you have a heavy loan with an interest of 12%, the bank is effectively taking 80% of your hard work (12 out of 15). You are doing 100% of the work, but keeping only "successful-looking" businesses suddenly go bankrupt because they were working for the bank all along.

9.6 The Consequences of Losing the Game

If the "Loan Game" goes wrong, the fall is not just financial; it is personal.

- **The Debt Spiral:** To pay the interest on Loan A, you take Loan B. To pay Loan B, you take a private loan. This is a hole that has no bottom.
- **The "CIBIL" Scar:** Once you miss a few payments, your credit score (CIBIL) is ruined. In the future, even if you have a great business idea, no bank will give you a single rupee.
- **Asset Seizure:** Most business loans are backed by "Collateral" (your shop, your home or your warehouse). If you can't pay back the loan, the bank can take possession of your property to recover its money. You don't just lose your business; you lose your family's roof.
- **Reputation Loss:** In the wholesale market, "news travels fast." Once people know you are struggling with bank payments, your suppliers will stop giving you credit, and your customers will start demanding lower prices because they know you are desperate for cash.

9.7 Conclusion: Be the Master, Not the Slave

A loan is a powerful fuel—it can help you reach your goals faster, but it is highly flammable.

The Merchant's Rule of Thumb: Use a loan to bridge **a Time Gap** (waiting for a customer to pay), but never to bridge a **Loss Gap** (Covering up for a business that isn't making a profit).

The goal of your business should eventually become "Debt-Free." Every rupee you save in interest is a rupee added directly to your family's wealth.

Play the loan game to scale, play it with discipline, and always have an exit plan.

Chapter 10
The Profit Puzzle – Understanding EBIDTA

10.1 Introduction: The "Rich" Counter vs. the "Poor" Bank Account

Have you ever had a month where your shop was constantly crowded, the cash drawer was overflowing, and you felt like a king? But then, at the end of the month, after paying the bank interest, the government, and the suppliers, you looked at your personal savings and wondered, "Where did it all go?"

This is the biggest mystery in the life of a merchant. To solve it, we need to understand a term that big corporations use, called **EBIDTA.**

Now, don't let the long name scare you. In simple "bazaar" language, EBIDTA is just your **"Shop's Core Strength."** It is the profit you make from buying and selling before the "outside world" (the banks and the government) and your "old equipment" take their share.

In this chapter, we will break down the journey of a single rupee. From the moment it enters your cash drawer to the moment it actually becomes yours to keep

10.2 The Story of the Two Warehouses

To understand this, let's look at two wholesalers, Manas and Sameer. Both sell the same hardware goods. Both have a turnover of Rs 1 crore.

Manas has a high-tech warehouse with expensive automated forklifts and a massive bank loan.

His "Shop Profit" (EBIDTA) is **Rs 15 Lakhs**. But because he has a huge loan, he pays Rs 8 Lakhs in **Interest.** Because his expensive machines are getting old, he has to set aside Rs 4 Lakhs for **Depreciation** (replacing them later). After **Taxes,** Manas is left with only **Rs 2 Lakhs** for himself.

Sameer runs a simple warehouse. He uses manual trolleys and has no bank loans. His "Shop Profit" (EBIDTA) is lower, only **Rs 10 Lakhs.** But because he has no interest to pay and very little depreciation, he pays his taxes and keeps **Rs 7 Lakhs** for himself.

The Lesson: Manas looks "Bigger" and "Busier," but Sameer is the one who is actually getting "Rich."

10.3 Breaking Down the "Bucket": What is EBIDTA?

Imagine your business is a large bucket.

- **The Water Coming in:** This is your sales (Revenue).
- **The First Holes in the Bucket:** These are your "Operational Costs"- The Cost of Buying stock, paying shop/warehouse rent, staff salaries, and electricity.

The water that remains in the bucket after these daily expenses is your **EBIDTA.** It shows how good you are at your trade. **If your EBIDTA is high, your "Trading Heart" is healthy.** But before you take that water home, there are four more "leaks" you must account for.

10.4 The Four Leaks: I, T, D and A.

Leak 1: Interest (The "I")

This is the "rent" you pay to the bank for using their money. As we discussed in the "Loan Game" chapter, interest is a silent partner that eats your profit twenty-four hours a day, even when you sleep.

- **Merchant's Tip:** If your interest is in eating more than 20% of your EBIDTA, your business is working for the bank, not for you.

Leak 2: Taxes (The "T")

The Government is your mandatory partner. Whether it is Income Tax or other levies, a portion of your hard work belongs to the nation.

- **Merchant's Tip:** Smart tax planning (with a CA) helps you keep more of your EBIDTA, but never ignore this leak, or it will turn into a flood of penalties later.

Leak 3: Depreciation (The "D")

This is a "hidden" leak. When you buy a delivery truck for Rs 10 Lakhs, it doesn't stay worth Rs 10 Lakhs. Every year, its value drops. If the truck lasts five years, you are losing Rs 2 Lakhs of value every year.

- **Merchant's Tip:** even if you aren't paying cash for it today, you must remember that one day that truck (or computer, or AC) will need to be replaced. If you don't account for this "Old Age" cost, you will have no money to buy a new one when the old one breaks.

Leak 4: Amortisation (The "A")

This is an Intangible Cost. This is similar to depreciation, but for things you can't touch, like a high-priced 10-year lease for a prime shop location or a software licence. You paid a big amount upfront, and its value is slowly "expiring" every year.

10.5 The "Real Profit" (The Bottom Line)

Once you **subtract** the **I, T, D and A** from your **EBIDTA,** you reach the **Net Profit (Profit After Tax).**

This is your true success. This is the money that can actually go into your family's gold, your children's education, or your personal savings.

As a merchant, you must focus on the "Bottom Line," not just the "Top Line" (Sales). Increasing your sales is useless if your Interest and Depreciation are eating everything up.

10.6 How to Make Your "Real Profit" Grow

To keep more money in your pocket, you have two choices:

1. Plug the Daily Holes: Negotiate better prices with suppliers and reduce electricity/staff waste to increase your EBIDTA.
2. Plug the Financial Leaks:
    - Reduce your high-interest loans.
    - Don't buy expensive machinery or vehicles unless they guarantee a massive increase in sales.
    - Maintain your equipment so it doesn't depreciate or break down faster than it should.

10.7 Conclusion: The Merchant's Reality Check

Don't be fooled by a busy shop. A merchant with a small, efficient shop and no loans is often wealthier than a wholesaler with a massive warehouse and a mountain of debt.

The Golden Rule of the Profit Puzzle: EBIDTA tells you how good your shop is. Net Profit tells you how good your business life will be.

Stop looking only at the cash counter. Start looking at what is left after the bank, the government and the "wear and tear" of life have taken their share. That is the only number that truly matters.

Chapter 11

Business Health Check: Financial Ratios Simplified

11.1 Introduction: Your Business's Blood Pressure and Sugar Levels

Imagine you go to a doctor for a check-up. The doctor doesn't just look at you and say, "You look fine." They take your blood pressure, check your sugar levels, and look at your heart rate. These are numbers that tell the truth about your health, even if you feel okay on the outside.

In your business, **financial ratios** are exactly like those health reports.

Many merchants make the mistake of looking only at their "Total Sales" or "Cash in Hand." But these numbers can be deceiving. A merchant doing Rs 1 crore in sales might be "unhealthy," while a merchant doing Rs 20 lakhs might be "fit."

Ratios help you compare two different numbers to see the real story. They turn a 50-page ledger into four or five simple numbers that tell you if your business is growing, standing still, or secretly dying.

11.2 The Tale of Two Brothers: The "Fast" and The "Full"

Two brothers, Amit and Sumit, inherited two identical garment shops.

Amit was obsessed with having a "full" shop. He kept every variety of cloth. His shop always looked impressive. He did Rs 50 Lakhs in sales, but his warehouse was packed with Rs 40 Lakhs worth of stock.

Amit's Ratio: His stock moved only **1.2 times** a year. His money was "stuck" in the cloth.

Sumit kept only the latest trends. His shop looked "thin" compared to Amit's. He also did Rs 50 Lakhs in sales, but he only kept Rs 5 Lakhs worth of stock at any time.

Sumit's Ratio: His stock moved **10 times** a year. He used the same over and over again to make a profit.

Even though their sales were the same, Sumit became a wealthy man while Amit struggled to pay his electricity bills. **Ratios showed the difference that sales couldn't.**

11.3 The Four Vital Signs: Ratios Every Merchant Must Track

A. **A. The "Speedometer": Stock Turnover Ratio**

This tells you how many times your stock "clears out" and is replaced in a year.

- **The Math:** Total Sales + Average Stock in Hand
- **Why it Matters:** If this number is **high**, it means your money is working. If it is **low,** it means your money is "sleeping" on the shelves.

- **Target:** For a merchant, you want this to be as high as possible. If it's dropping, it means you are buying things your customers don't want.

B. **The "Fuel Gauge": Current Ratio**

This tells you if you have enough "liquid" strength to pay your bills for the next 12 months.

- **The Math:** What you Own (Cash + Stock + Trade Receivables) **divided by** What you Owe (Supplier bills + Short-term loans)
- **Why it Matters:** A healthy ratio is usually **2:1.** This means for every Rs 1 you owe, you have Rs 2 in resources.
- **Warning:** If this falls below 1:1, you are in the "Danger Zone." You might not be able to pay your suppliers tomorrow morning.

C. **The "Reward": Net Profit Margin**

This tells you how much money you actually keep for every Rs 1 of Sales.

- **The Math:** Net Profit/Total Sales x 100
- **Why it Matters:** Many wholesalers work on a thin margin. For example, if a wholesaler is working on 2% margin and if your expenses rise by even 1%, half your profit is gone.
- **Warning:** If your sales are increasing but this ratio is decreasing, you are "running faster just to stay in the same place." You are working harder for less reward.

D. **The "Ownership": Debt to Equity Ratio**

This tells you who really owns your business — You or the Bank?

- **The Math:** Total Loans **divided by** Your Own Capital (Investment + Savings)
- **Why it Matters:** If this is **too high,** you are a "slave" to interest. If the market slows down, the bank will take your shop.
- **Target:** Try to keep your own capital higher than your loans.

11.4 The Consequences of "Bad" Ratios:

When these numbers go out of balance, the impact is like a slow-acting poison.

1. **Invisible Bankruptcy:** You might feel successful because customers are buying, but a bad **Current Ratio** means you are one "delayed payment" away from shutting down.
2. **Profit Leakage:** A bad **Stock Turnover** means you are paying interest on loans to fund stock that nobody is buying.
3. **Bank Rejection:** When you go for a loan to expand, the bank doesn't look at your shop's decoration; they look at these ratios. If the ratios are bad, the bank will say "No," even if you are a "big name" in the market.
4. **Operational Stress:** Bad Ratios lead to "firefighting." You spend your day juggling money instead of growing the business.

11.5 Why Ratios are Your Best Friend

Ratios allow you to:

- **Compare Yourself to Last Year:** "Am I more efficient than I was last year?"
- **Compare Yourself to Competitors:** "Why is the shop next door growing faster with the same stock?"
- **Spot Trouble Early:** Ratios act like an "Early Warning System." They show the problem six months before the cash actually runs out.

11.6 Conclusion: Be the Doctor of Your Own Business

You don't need a degree in finance to understand your business health. You only need to check these four to five numbers once a month.

The Merchant's Checklist:

- Is my stock moving faster than last month? **(Stock Turnover Ratio)**
- Can I pay all my suppliers twice over if I had to? **(Current Ratio)**
- Am I keeping enough money from every sale? **(Net Margin Ratio)**
- Do I own more of this business than the bank does? **(Debt to Equity Ratio)**

If the answer to these is "Yes," your business is fit. If the answer is "No," it doesn't matter how big your shop is- it's time for a "Financial Surgery."

Chapter 12

Tax Planning–Winning the Game, Not Breaking the Rules

12.1 Introduction: The "Year-End Fever"

Every year, as the month of March approaches, a strange "fever" grips the market. Merchants stop focusing on sales and start running to their accountants with bags full of random bills. They are desperate to "save tax."

In the world of trade, tax is often seen as a "loss" or a "penalty" for being successful. But as a smart merchant, you must change your perspective. Tax is a Business Expense, just like rent or electricity. If you plan your electricity usage, you save on the bill. If you plan your business transactions, you save on the tax bill—legally and safely.

However, there is a very thin line between being "Smart" and being a "Criminal." In this chapter, we will learn how to navigate the world of taxes without losing your sleep or your reputation.

12.2 The Story of the Two Neighbours: The "Hider" vs. The "Planner"

In a busy wholesale market, two friends, Rajesh and Sunil, ran similar distribution businesses.

Rajesh believed in "Hiding." He did a lot of unrecorded ("kacha") Sales. He didn't keep proper bills for his expenses. He thought he was very smart because his "On-Paper" profit was zero, and he paid zero tax.

- The Result: When Rajesh wanted to buy a bigger warehouse to expand his business, the bank rejected his loan. Why? Because on paper, his business was "making no money." He was stuck in a small shop forever.

Sunil believed in "Planning." He recorded every sale. He sat with his advisor every quarter. He used legal deductions for his office equipment, his insurance and his home loan.

- The Result: Sunil paid some tax, but his "book of accounts" was strong. The bank saw his steady growth and gave him a Rs 1 crore loan easily. Sunil moved to a massive warehouse and doubled his turnover.

The Lesson: Rajesh saved a few thousand in tax but lost lakhs in growth. Sunil used tax planning as a ladder to success.

12.3 Tax Planning vs. Tax Evasion: Know the Difference

This is the most important distinction you will ever learn in business.

- **Tax Planning (The Smart Way):** This is using the **Rules of the Game** to your advantage.
- The Government wants you to invest in new machinery, save for your retirement, and buy insurance. When you do these things, they give you a "discount" on your taxes. This is 100% legal and highly encouraged.
- **Tax Evasion (The Dangerous Way):** This is **Breaking the Rules.** Hiding sales, creating "fake" expense bills, or

keeping two sets of books. This is a crime. It leads to heavy penalties, raids and can even land a merchant in jail.

Merchan's Rule: Planning is like using a coupon code for a discount; Evasion is like shoplifting.

12.4 Why Tax Planning is a "Success Tool"

Why should you spend time on this?

1. **Cash Flow Control:** Taxes are often paid in large chunks (Advance Tax). If you don't plan, you might face a sudden "Cash Crunch" in September or March.
2. **Wealth Creation:** Instead of giving money to the government as a penalty, planning helps you to divert that money into productive investments (like a PPF, Insurance, or new Business Assets).
3. **Bankability:** As we saw with Sunil, "clean" books make you a favourite for banks. You can get loans at lower interest rates.
4. **Peace of Mind:** You can sit in your shop with your head held high, knowing that no government notice can shake your foundation.

12.5 The "Big Blunders" Merchants Make

Most merchants don't "plan," they "react." Here are the common mistakes:

- **The "March 31st" Panic:** Trying to "fix" everything in the last week of the year. Real tax planning starts on April 1st.

- **Mixing Personal and Business:** Using the shop's cash to pay for a cousin's wedding or a personal vacation, and trying to show it as a "Business Expenditure." This is a red flag for the tax officers.
- **Ignoring Advance Tax:** Many traders think, "I will pay all the tax at the end of the year." But the law requires you to pay in instalments. But ignoring this, you end up paying 12%–15% extra in interest and penalties for no reason.
- **The "Kacha-Pakka" Trap:** Selling without a bill. This not only risks a GST raid but also makes your business "un-sellable" and "in-loanable" in the future.

12.6 How to Plan Like a Professional

You don't need to be an expert; you just need to be organised.

1. **Choose the Right Structure:** (Remember Chapter 1.) Sometimes, moving from a Proprietorship to a Company can save you a lot of tax as your turnover grows.
2. **Claim Every "Real" Expense:** Ensure your tea/coffee bills for customers, your staff's mobile recharges, your vehicle fuel and even your home office internet are billed in the business name. These are legal deductions.
3. **Use Depreciation Wisely:** If you need a new computer or a delivery van, buy it before the year ends so you can claim the "wear and tear" (depreciation) as an expense to reduce your taxable profit.
4. **Invest in Your Future:** Use applicable sections in the Income Tax Act to invest in life/health insurance. You are protecting your family and reducing your tax at the same time.

12.7 Conclusion: Don't work for the Taxman

A merchant who doesn't plan for taxes is like a bucket with a hole at the bottom. No matter how much "Sales" water you pour in, the money will keep leaking out.

Tax planning is not about "cheating" the government; it is about being an Efficient Merchant. When you plan well, you keep more of your hard-earned profit, you build a stronger reputation, and you ensure that your business stays on the path of "Success" for generations.

The Golden Rule:

Pay every paisa of tax that is due, but not a single paisa that can be legally saved.

Chapter 13
Small Adjustments, Big Scrutiny.

13.1 Introduction: The "Little Adjustment" Trap.

In the bustling markets of our cities, there is a word often whispered among merchants: "Adjustment."

It sounds harmless, doesn't it? A small "adjustment" in the stock value, a little "adjustment" in the cash sales, or a tiny "adjustment" in a fuel bill. Many wholesalers and retailers believe that these minor shortcuts are the secret to saving money and staying ahead of the competition. They think, "The government is looking for the big fish; they won't notice my small changes."

But in today's digital world, there is no such thing as a "small" adjustment. What you see as a clever shortcut, the tax department sees as a **red flag.**

In this chapter, we will explore why these "small" illegal moves are a ticking time bomb for your business and why a professional advisor is your best shield against a disaster you didn't see coming.

13.2 The Story of Mr. Gupta: The Man with the "Perfect" Books

Mr. Gupta was a successful distributor of electronics. He was proud of himself because he never paid "too much" tax. Every month, he would sit with his accountant and say, "Add Rs 50,000 to the repaid expenses," or "Show this personal family trip as a "Business Conference."

He felt invincible. For five years, nothing happened. He saved about Rs 2 Lakhs in tax every year. He felt like a genius.

Then, on a quiet Tuesday morning, a notice arrived. It wasn't about a major fraud; it was a **data-mismatch scrutiny.** The tax department's computer had noticed that while Mr. Gupta's sales were growing by 20%, his "Repairs and Maintenance" expenses had jumped by 400%.

The "Small Adjustment" led to a Deep Scrutiny of the last six years.

- **The Adjustment Savings:** Rs 12 Lakh. (Over 6 years)
- **The Penalty and Interest:** Rs 35 Lakhs
- **The Legal Fees:** Rs 5 Lakhs
- **The Result:** Mr. Gupta had to sell his delivery van and take a loan just to pay the government. His "smartness" cost him his peace of mind and his business growth.

13.3 The Five "Silent Alarms" That Trigger Scrutiny

In the past, scrutiny was a matter of luck. Today, it is a matter of data. The government's systems are now linked. Here are the five specific "alarms" that most merchants accidentally trigger.

A. **The Turnover Mismatch (GST vs. Income Tax):** This is the most common blunder. The GST and Income Tax Departments now share data instantly. If your turnover in one doesn't match the other to the last paisa, a "Mismatch Notice" is automatically generated by the system.

B. **The AIS Mismatch (The Government's "Secret Diary"):** Every merchant has an **AIS (Annual Information Statement).** Think of this as the government's diary of your life. It records your high-value credit card spends, your fixed deposit interest, your property purchases, and even your share market trades.

C. **The Cash Deposit "Galla" Trap:** Many traders believe that depositing cash into their business or savings account in small chunks won't be noticed. If you deposit cash without a corresponding sales bill, the tax department can treat that entire amount as "unexplained income" and tax it at a massive rate, which can go up to 100% plus penalties.

D. **The "Fake" Unsecured Loans:** When a merchant needs money but doesn't want to show it as profit, they often show "Unsecured Loans" from friends or relatives in their books. But the Tax Department now looks deeply into the identity, capacity, and genuineness of the person giving the loan. In the absence of it, that loan will be added to the merchant's income, and he will face the heat.

E. **The Low GP (Gross Profit) Ratio:** Every trader has a standard profit margin. If every other cloth wholesaler in your market makes a 10% Gross Profit, but you show only 2%, the system flags you. A consistently low GP Ratio compared to the market is a direct invitation for an audit.

13.4 The Digital Eye: Why You Can No Longer Hide

Ten years ago, the tax department was a room full of dusty files. Today, it is a **supercomputer.**

If you are a merchant, you must realise that the GST Department, the Income Tax Department, and even your Bank are all "talking" to each other through Artificial Intelligence (AI).

- If you buy a luxury car, the Income Tax Department knows.
- If your GST sales don't match your Income Tax Return, a red flag is raised instantly.
- If your electricity bill for the warehouse is very high, but you show "zero production or sales," the system knows you are hiding stock.

The Reality: The era of "Small Adjustments" is over. You are living in a glass house, and the taxman has a telescope.

13.5 The Real Impact of Scrutiny (The Hidden Losses)

Most merchants only think about the "Tax Amount." But the real loss of tax scrutiny is much deeper.

1. **The Time Drain:** A Scrutiny can last for months or even years. Instead of focusing on your sales and finding new distributors, you spend your days in a CA's office or answering government queries. Your business suffers because the captain (you) is distracted.
2. **The "CIBIL" and Bank Damage:** Once you are under scrutiny for a tax "adjustment," banks become very nervous. They may freeze your Current/Savings/CC Accounts or refuse to give you a loan for expansion. Your growth stops.
3. **The Interest Snowball:** Tax penalties in India are heavy (often 100% to 200% of the tax avoided), but the Interest (usually

12%–18%) is what truly kills the business. It keeps ticking every single day from the date the tax was originally due.

4. **Reputation Loss:** In the trade market, credit is built on trust. If the news spreads that your warehouse was inspected or your accounts are under scrutiny, your suppliers might stop giving you credit, and your business will suffocate.

13.6 Why You Need an Advisor, Not an "Adjuster"

Many merchants treat their accountant like a magician who should "make the tax disappear." This is a recipe for disaster.

A Professional Tax Advisor **(Chartered Accountant)** is like a **GPS for your business.**

- An Adjuster will tell you how to hide a mistake today, only to see you fall into a hole tomorrow.
- An Advisor will tell you not to do this. Instead, they will advise you to use the legal deductions to naturally lower your taxes.

The Advantage of an Advisor:

- They keep you updated on the latest rules.
- They act as a "Buffer" between you and the department.
- They help you build a "Clean Balance Sheet" that you can proudly show to a bank to get a loan.

13.7 The "Golden Rule" for the Modern Merchant

Don't be **"Penny Wise and Pound Foolish."**

Saving Rs 10,000 by making a fake entry is like saving a drop of water while your whole tank is leaking. If you want to build a business that lasts for 50 years and can be passed to your children, it must be built on a foundation of **Trust.**

How to Stay Safe:

1. **Record Every Transaction:** Even the small ones.
2. **Separate Personal from Business:** Never pay for your home groceries from the shop's account.
3. **Invest in Professional Advice:** Paying a fee to a good CA is an **Investment**, not an expense. It is the premium you pay for your business's "Life Insurance."

13.8 Conclusion: Sleep Better, Scale Bigger

A merchant who makes "Small Adjustments" lives in constant fear of a phone call or a knock on the door. A merchant who follows the rules and has a good advisor lives with a clear mind.

The Merchant's Motto:

If you can't explain it to an officer with a smile on your face, don't put it in your books.

Chapter 14

Beyond the Signature - Your CA as a Partner in Success.

14.1 Introduction: From "Tax Filer" to "Growth Partner"

For many merchants, a Chartered Accountant is someone they call once a month for GST or once a year for an Income Tax Return. They see the CA as a "Necessity Cost"- someone who keeps the government away so they can focus on their business.

But if you only use your CA for compliance, you are using a Ferrari to go to the grocery store. You are missing out on 90% of the value.

In this final chapter, we will look at how a CA can move from being a "Scorekeeper" (someone who tells you what happened yesterday) to a "Coach" (someone who helps you win tomorrow). Your CA should not just be your auditor; they should be your strategic partner in building a **legacy of success.**

4.2 The Story of the Two Distributors: One Alone, One Advised.

Imagine two distributors, Mitesh and Ritesh, both running large warehouses with similar turnovers.

Mitesh calls his CA only when a notice arrives or a deadline is near. He makes all his business decisions, like buying new stock, opening a branch, or taking a loan, based on his "gut feeling."

One year, Mitesh realised too late that while his sales were up, his bank interest was eating 80% of his profit. He was working hard, but his wealth was shrinking.

Ritesh meets his CA every month. Before he buys a new warehouse, he asks his CA to check the **feasibility.** Before he takes a loan, his CA calculates **the ROI (Return on Investment).**

Because Ritesh has a professional advisor by his side, he avoided a bad expansion and negotiated a better credit limit with his bank.

Mitesh is struggling to survive; Ritesh is scaling his empire. The difference wasn't the market, but it was the advice.

14.3 Reviews and Meetings

In the fast-moving world of trade, a year is too long to wait for a "Health Check."

- **Monthly Reviews:** A CA can sit with you every 30 days to review your Gross Profit (GP) Ratio, your Stock Turnover, and your Expense Trends.
- **Course Correction:** If your margins dropped by 2% this month, a monthly review catches it now. If you only check at the end of the year, you have already lost 12 months of profit.

14.4 Risk Detection: Your Business's "Security Guard."

A merchant is often too busy with customers to notice internal leaks. A CA adds value by acting as a "Risk Detector."

- **Inventory Leaks:** Identifying "Dead Stock" or unexplained shortages in the warehouse.
- **Fraud Prevention:** Setting up a system so that staff can't easily siphon off cash or stock.
- **Compliance Risk:** Catching a GST Mismatch before the department sends a notice. This saves you from heavy penalties that can be more than your annual profit.

14.5 Cash Flow Planning and Strategic Advisory

As we discussed in previous chapters, "Cash is King." Your CA helps you manage the **timing of money.**

- **Cash Flow Forecasting:** Helping you plan for months where you need extra capital for festive stock.
- **Strategic Growth:** Should you buy a shop or continue on rent? Should you add a new product line? A CA doesn't just look at the "price"; they look at the "payback period." They help you make decisions based on **Data,** not just **Emotion.**

14.6 The Virtual CFO (Chief Financial Officer): Big Company Brain for Your Small Business.

You might not be able to hire a full-time Finance Director worth lakhs of rupees, but you can have a **Virtual CFO.**

- This is where your CA takes over the entire financial strategy of your business. They help with bank negotiations, cost-cutting measures, and performance tracking.
- They ensure that your "Back Office" is as strong as your "Front Counter."

14.7 Tax Planning Over Tax Evasion: Building a Clean Legacy

This is the most critical value a CA adds. As we have seen, "adjustments" lead to scrutiny.

- **The High Road:** A CA guides you on how to use Depreciation, Business Deductions and Investment Schemes to lower your tax legally.
- **The Result:** You build a "Clean Balance Sheet." When a bank sees a business that is transparent and well-planned, they offer lower interest rates and higher limits. Your "Tax Planning" becomes your "Growth Tool."

14.8 Conclusion: The Foundation of Your Success

My dear merchant friends, the journey of Stock, Sales and Success is not a solo journey. The most successful traders in the world have one thing in common: they have a trusted financial advisor by their side.

Don't look at your CA as an "Annual Expense." Look at them as an **Asset.**

- If they help you reduce your interest by 1%, they have paid for their fee.

- If they prevent a single tax penalty, they have saved your reputation.
- If they help you scale from one shop to five, they have changed your family's future.

The Merchant's Final Rule:

Focus on what you do best – Trading.

Let your CA do what they do best – Protecting and growing your wealth.

Together, you are UNSTOPPABLE.

www.ingramcontent.com/pod-product-compliance
Lightning Source LLC
LaVergne TN
LVHW050922210926
848482LV00012B/502